PARADISE TAKEN

PARADISE
THE DIARY OF EDEN FLORES PART I
TAKEN

OMAR GONZALEZ

Rise Above Publishing LLC
Kansas City, MO

PARADISE TAKEN
The Diary of Eden Flores
Copyright © 2021 by Omar Gonzalez

Cover design by Lance Buckley

First Rise Above Publishing edition - July 2021

Paperback ISBN: 978-1-7356242-3-5

This book is also available in these additional formats:
Hardcover ISBN: 978-1-7356242-2-8
Ebook ISBN: 978-1-7356242-4-2

Library of Congress Control Number: 2021901019

Rise Above Publishing LLC
Kansas City, MO

*For
the Victims,
the Survivors,
and the
Courageous*

CONTENTS

"Child sexual abuse is a significant but preventable public health problem. Many children wait to report or never report child sexual abuse."

"About 1 in 4 girls and 1 in 13 boys experience child sexual abuse at some point in childhood."

"91% of child sexual abuse is perpetrated by someone the child or child's family knows."

For more information, please visit:
https://www.cdc.gov/violenceprevention/
childabuseandneglect/childsexualabuse.html

If you suspect a child to be the victim of sexual abuse, please call the **Darkness to Light** Hotline:
866.FOR.LIGHT (866.367.5444)

"On average, nearly 20 people per minute are physically abused by an intimate partner in the United States. During one year, this equates to more than 10 million women and men."

"1 in 15 children are exposed to intimate partner violence each year, and 90% of these children are eyewitnesses to this violence."

For more information, please visit:
https://www.ncadv.org

If you or anyone you believe may need help, please call The National Domestic Violence Hotline:
1-800-799 SAFE (7233)
or go online to
https://www.DomesticShelters.org

PARADISE

THE DIARY OF EDEN FLORES PART I

TAKEN

OMAR GONZALEZ

PREFACE

The stories in this diary are true. The events described in it took place during Eden Flores's childhood. Although not written by Eden, the stories and poems in this book follow her perspective.

INTRODUCTION

I was five years old when I first visited my parents' native country of El Salvador. Like most children that age, I was unaware of what exactly to expect. All my parents told me was that I would be far from home and that I was there to visit family I had never met before. Honestly, I looked forward to seeing El Salvador. My mom would always tell me many fun stories about her childhood, especially about the town where she had grown up, El Paraiso ("Paradise"). My mother's demeanor would change whenever she spoke about El Paraiso. I could always feel the pride and joy she exuded when she told me about her life growing up in El Paraiso. However, once there, I did not see the paradise my mother spoke of so proudly.

Instead, I saw a place in chaos, ruled by violence and fear. All around me, there were men dressed in green outfits, walking around with big guns. Dirty children sped by, running barefoot on the hot pavement, trying to sell whatever they could to whoever would buy. Most of the women I saw walked around carrying piles of pots and bags on top of their heads. The roads were bumpy and nothing like streets I was accustomed to in the United States. Although we were in the place my mother had called home for so many years, we did not stay long as most of my mother's family had left El Paraiso.

The next place we headed to was the town where my father grew up, Ahuachapán. We drove for what felt like an eternity, but eventually arrived just before dusk. Once there, members from my father's side of the family greeted us. I must have met about thirty people that night; at least that was what it had felt like to me. However, the person who astonished me the most was my grandmother, more specifically her mustache. It reminded me of Captain Hook's mustache from the Peter Pan movie I loved so much. I thought to myself, Is she my grandmother or my grandfather?

The longer we stayed there, the more out of place I remember feeling. I could not help it; everything I saw just confused me. The oven was powered not by electricity but by burning wood. The toilet paper was equivalent to sandpaper, and the men of the household would take a big barrel down to the nearby river and fill it with water. Once the men retrieved the water, it was then carefully rationed to prevent frequent trips to get more. Notably, using the bathroom consisted of walking outside, about fifty feet from the house, to a creepy-looking outhouse where one had to either stand or squat over a hole in the ground. If someone wanted to take a hot shower, at least what resembled a shower, they had to boil the water beforehand.

During my time there, I learned hard lessons in being frugal as anything that I did that involved water, food, or household supplies always resulted in people yelling at me or slapping my hands very hard.

The only good memory I have of the entire trip was the day I spent at the market with my grandmother. She owned a small stand there where she sold things that, I thought at the time, looked to be in the potato family. My grandmother knew most of the other stand owners at the market, so she paraded me around and told them I was her granddaughter from the United States. To my surprise, a lot of them gave me candy, food, and small toys, and they could not stop saying how pretty I was. Up to that point in my life, no one had ever spoiled me like that, and so not wanting to lose that moment,

I kept walking around the market, seeing what I could get from people.

After numerous rounds of walking around and about the market, I finally had enough. My feet ached, my skin had taken a beating from the sun, and my stomach felt so full that I thought it would pop. I decided to take a break at my grandmother's stand, where I sat on a tall stool and watched everyone go about their business. As I sat there looking, one thing that had caught my attention was the number of children my age working there at the market.

I turned to my grandmother and asked, "Hey, Grandma, why are all of these kids here and not in school?"

Although my understanding of Spanish at the time was not as good as it is today, I am convinced she said, "These kids have to work to survive. Parents here don't raise a bunch of spoiled crybabies the way Americans do. Look at you, even here, these poor people spoil you because you're from the United States. They think that you must be royalty. But the truth is, you're not. Don't ever think that you're something special!"

I listened in silence, wondering why she had become so angry with me.

While I sat there, two boys, who seemed older than me, walked over toward my grandmother. "Celia, do you know if our dad will be coming here today?" they asked my grandmother.

Suddenly, the expression on her face changed from angry to furious rage. "Get the fuck out of here, you two good-for-nothing bastards, before I beat the shit out of you!" she yelled as she kicked one of them in the backside and chased them off.

Filled with fear, I just sat there and did not even think to ask her who they were or why she had done what she did.

As sunset drew near, I helped my grandmother close up the shop. Before beginning our walk back home, she placed what looked like a rolled-up towel on my head, followed by a pot. Quickly, she taught me a short lesson on balancing a pot on my head as I walked. Although I was happy that I quickly picked up the technique, I was not comfortable having to walk back the entire way, balancing something on my head. Walking down the path we had traveled that morning, I suddenly became confused when my grandmother veered off the course and began to follow another trail.

"Your father asked me to take you to meet your great grandmother," said my grandmother with an annoyed tone. "We'll stop by, say hello, and then we're out of there."

As we neared the house, we were met outside by a very old-looking woman with a hunched back.

Once we had come within arm's reach of my great grandmother, my grandmother said, "Josefina, look. This is my granddaughter, Carlos's daughter."

Admittedly, my great-grandmother was frightening, so I stood still, not knowing what to do.

"Oh, my God, you are the most beautiful girl I've ever seen," she said as she embraced me ever so tightly. "God has blessed you but also cursed you."

After being comforted by her, I became less intimidated.

"Okay, well, we have to go now," said Celia as she picked up her bags and began to walk toward the path.

"Wait, wait!" shouted Josefina at Celia. "I have to give the little princess something; just wait," she demanded as she walked into her home.

My grandmother gave me an uneasy look as both of us stood, waiting for my great grandmother. Hearing the door open, I turned to see my great grandmother walk toward me with a long and sharp knife.

She knelt in front of me, opened my hand, placed the knife in it, and said, "You're going to need this. You're just too beautiful. One day soon, you'll need to use this."

My first unforgettable gift.

CHAPTER 1

HIDE & SEEK

Nina, such a lovable and caring golden retriever with a beautiful golden coat, was a perfect match for my brothers and me when we were young kids. At least, that was what I thought before Dad said we couldn't afford to provide for Nina's care and gave her away. Luckily for my brothers and me, Nina was adopted by a lovely young couple, Mitch and Jenny, who allowed us to visit her as often as we wanted. We came to enjoy going over to their apartment to play with Nina, and they also grew to enjoy having us over. Admittedly, we would try to spend as much time at their place as possible—it was a nice escape from the chaos my father created at home.

When thinking back to that time, I honestly cannot remember when my father was not calling my mother a pig, bitch, disgusting, fat, dumb, piece of shit, or several other derogatory phrases he had for her. He did not allow her to work, learn English, or dress nicely. Her primary role in life was to serve him at all times, even above my brothers and me. We, too, had similar positions, especially me. Still, there were two universal rules that everyone in his household had to abide by: only speak when spoken to and never challenge his authority. Any of us who did not follow those rules would suffer severe physical consequences. One could see why we loved spending so much time at Mitch and Jenny's place.

Although Mitch and Jenny were both so kind to us, Mitch captured my attention the most. He was so sweet to his wife and never mistreated her. Mitch often hugged Jenny and told her that she was beautiful. He was also very attentive and never took issue with helping around the house. When it came to my brothers and me, Mitch was patient and kind. I always felt at ease at their place as there was no tension or need to fear consequences always. During that time, I often wished that Mitch and Jenny would adopt us as well.

One breezy but beautiful summer day, Mitch and Jenny invited us to spend the day with them at the enormous inground pool of their apartment complex. It was such a wonderful experience as all of us spent the day playing pool games, splashing each other, laughing, eating hotdogs and hamburgers for lunch, and drifting idly on floaties afterward. As I floated around the pool on my floaty, I could not help but wish for the day to never end. Although the fun and the love I experienced at the pool on that day was something I was not familiar with, I hoped to encounter more of it. As the day winded down, we all headed inside to dry off and get ready for dinner.

While Jenny prepared dinner, she realized that she was missing a few critical ingredients for what she wanted to cook. So, she announced that she was going to the grocery store and asked my brothers and me if we wanted to tag along. My brothers said "yes" but I said "no." I wished to stay behind to play with Nina. As Jenny and my brothers left to go to the store, Mitch closed the door behind them. He then turned to look at me as I sat in the living room, petting Nina.

"Hey, how about a game of hide and seek?" he asked me.

I remember becoming excited because I enjoyed playing that game with my brothers. So I said, "yes."

He replied, "Okay, I'll hide first. Close your eyes and count to thirty, really slow, and then come find me."

"Thirty, okay, here I come!" I shouted as I began to search the apartment for Mitch. I searched the living room, kitchen, office, guest bedroom, and bathroom but to no avail. Finally, I headed toward their bedroom. Once inside, I did not look far or long as I saw the light on from under the master bathroom door.

I remember thinking to myself, "Wow, Mitch made it too easy." So, I burst through the door and shouted, "Gotcha!"

However, my excitement ended abruptly as Mitch appeared before me, naked, touching his penis, and stepping in my direction.

CHAPTER 2

TACOS

Pennies

A nickel

A dime

A quarter!

"Okay, Alex, do we have enough?"

"No, Junior, we've only got fifty cents so far."

"Fuck!"

"Come on, Eden, stop cursing!"

"Hey, you and Alex curse all the time!"

"Yeah, but Alex and I are the ones who get punished
because of your cursing!"

"Hey, Junior, let's check out the laundry room?"

"Oh shit, yeah, good call, bro. Come on, Eden, let's go!"

Pennies

A nickel

A dime

Another quarter!

"Nice! Please tell me that we have a dollar."

"Not yet, Junior, we need one more penny."

"What? Oh, come on!"

"Juanito really won't take ninety-nine cents?
It's pretty much a dollar!"

"I don't think Juanito is that dude's name, Eden.
I'm pretty sure *Juanito's* is just the name of the..."

"Oh, shut up, Alex! And no, Eden, Alex and I tried that
last time. That dude is grimy as hell!"

"*Last time?* What do you mean *last time?*
You two have gone there without me?"

"Yes, Eden, we've gone there without you. But only when
dad takes you out to eat and leaves Alex and me behind.
What the hell are we supposed to do, wait for you to
come back to tell us about your good ol' time with dad?
Meanwhile, Alex and I haven't eaten jack shit!"

"Hey, it's not my fault that you two are always on his
shit list. Don't be mad at me; be mad at yourselves!"

"Why, you little..."

"Hey! Can you two shut the hell up already? We need
one damn penny! Come on. I'm hungry as hell!"

"Okay, we're done here. Let's go look outside."

Looking.

Looking.

"Look, a penny and dime!"

"Ha-ha, nice! Way to go, Junior!"

"Ow, come on, Alex, watch out!"

"What?"

"My back is still fucked up from yesterday."

"Oh, shit, I forgot, man. I'm sorry."

"How the hell can you forget something like that?
Dad beat my ass with a wire hanger!"

"Hey, man, if it's not my ass that he's whooping, I try not to
be around when he's whooping someone else's ass."

"Bro, he was fucking mom up. I had to do something!"

"Not for nothing, but I told you that jumping
in the middle was a bad idea."

"Whatever, man!"

"Hey! Are you two girls done chatting?
We getting tacos or what?"

CHAPTER 3

LIKE A BOY

Why do you dress

Like a boy?

Because dressing

Like a girl

Caused men

To look at me weird.

Why do you dress

Like a boy?

Because dressing

Like a girl

Caused men

To say weird things

To me.

Why do you dress

Like a boy?

Because dressing

Like a girl

Caused men

To touch me.

Why do you dress

Like a boy?

Because dressing

Like a girl

Caused my father

To beat me.

Why do you dress

Like a boy?

Because I thought

That if I looked

Like a boy,

Men would

Leave me alone.

But no matter

What I do,

Someone always

Makes fun of me,

Someone always

Gets mad at me,

Someone Always

Touches me.

CHAPTER 4

THE EXORCIST

If there is one aunt I will never forget, it would have to be my Aunt Maria, my mother's older sister. Although my brothers and I did not see much of her growing up, she made her presence exceptionally known and unforgettable to us the few times we did see her.

One summer, while my brothers and I stayed with our grandparents, my Aunt Maria decided that it was time to introduce us to God. She did so by taking us to church every Sunday and also enrolling us into the church's summer Bible camp. My brothers and I honestly came to enjoy Bible camp; it got us out of the house, took us on fun adventures, and we even got cool prizes when winning any of the many Bible-themed games. Unfortunately, the camp only lasted half of the summer, so once it was over, all we had left was going to church on Sundays.

Though we weren't against church as a concept, my brothers and I did not find it as entertaining as Bible camp. Consequently, telling my Aunt Maria that we were bored in the church was one big "no-no."

"Church is not supposed to be fun, you little heathens!" was her response to our displeasure.

I mean, it was not only that my brothers and I found the church to be boring; we honestly had no clue what the pastor was talking about most of the time. We were only kids then; how were we supposed to understand the complexities of the relationship between God and man? Even when the pastor happened to say something that caught our curiosity, asking my aunt about it after the church service was out of the question.

"How dare you question God? Your only role in life is to keep your mouth shut and listen to His word!" was her usual refrain to every one of our questions.

The only thing that kept Sunday church service somewhat entertaining was all of the church members' weird practices. It was not uncommon to walk into that church in the middle of service and find people passed out on the floor, shaking, crying, or speaking in tongues. For the folks not on the floor, one could see them running up, down, and around the aisles, shaking and gyrating their bodies as well speaking in tongues. Finding the behavior to be weird, my brothers and I had never participated in the past. Becoming fed up, my brothers and I devised a plan to ensure that the following Sunday church service would be our last.

The Sunday of all Sundays finally arrived. It was the middle of service, and like clockwork, the pastor started his routine. As he made his way around the pews, placing his hand on people's foreheads, my brothers and I shook in anticipation to enact our plan. Finally, there stood the pastor before us. First, he placed his hand on Junior's head, said a prayer and Junior was off!

Junior decided that he would run around the church screaming "Hallelujah" while doing cartwheels and jumping jacks for his performance.

Pleased with what he saw, the pastor then proceeded to place his hand upon Alex's head, say a prayer, and then Alex was off! Alex fell to the floor for his performance and did the worm up and down the aisle.

Becoming excited by the work of the Lord that he was witnessing before him, the pastor then proceeded to wrap his entire sweaty hand around my face. Upon saying the prayer, I forcefully threw myself back into the pew and began to convulse. I shook so hard it must have looked as if electricity was coursing through my body.

Filled with the Holy Spirit from watching my brothers and me, the pastor began loudly preaching, "You know, when I look at these kids who have become filled with the Holy Ghost, I can't help but feel good! I feel good because I know there's a God somewhere! There's a God somewhere! Turn around members and look at these wonderful children for me, please! You know there's a God when you see something like that! Only God can give these kids the kind of joy they have right there! Make a joyful noise unto the Lord!"

Suddenly, my Aunt Maria fell to her knees, threw up her arms, and shouted, "Yes, Lord, you have heard my prayers! Yes! Yes! Yes! Thank you, Lord, for saving these children!"

Once the craziness had passed, the pastor closed the service with a prayer. Back at our grandparent's home, my Aunt Maria could not stop bragging about how she was ultimately the one responsible for saving our souls. Unable to hold our composure, the three of us burst into laughter.

Confused by our outbreak, she asked, "Just what in the hell is so funny?"

"Bahahaha, we fooled you," answered Junior. "We fooled all of you! We were only acting."

Alex added, "We figured if we had to go to church, we might as well make it fun and entertaining."

Realizing that our performance during service had been one big mockery, my aunt became filled with wrath. She stormed to her room and came back with a medium-sized glass bottle and a leather strap. She forced us down onto our knees and made us take off our shirts. Once she had us kneeling on the floor shirtless, she then began to whip us and pour the contents from the bottle onto our raw skin. As she did so, she also shouted out verses from the Bible.

A half-hour passed, but she only became more fervent. She was intent on getting the devil out of us. I remember seeing the crimson on her cheeks. I had seen people get red in the face before, but this was different. It was as if she had been the one possessed.

"Get behind me, Satan!" she screamed from the top of her lungs. "Satan, leave these kids' bodies, come out of them. God commands you! I command you!" she kept on shouting.

No longer able to take what was happening, Junior stood up and said, "Fuck this. I'm out."

As soon as Junior turned his back, my aunt pounced on him like a lion on a gazelle! She tackled Junior so hard that the front of his head bounced off the floor. Lying there dazed and confused, she turned him over and began to choke him as if attempting to snuff the life out of a demon, literally.

Fearing for Junior's life, Alex and I jumped on her, hitting her, pulling her hair, and even biting her to no avail. She was going to strangle our brother to death, and we were helpless to stop it. Suddenly, out of nowhere, we saw a cane fly through the air and strike my aunt directly in the forehead. The cane hit her head so hard that it knocked her off Junior.

"What the fuck are you doing? Are you fucking crazy?" shouted my grandfather.

He then walked over to Junior to see if he was okay. Satisfied with Junior's well-being, my grandfather then instructed my brothers and me to go to our room and close the door. Once in our room, more shouting commenced in the living room.

My grandfather was not done with her as he shouted, "How dare you treat them like that? They are just kids. They need love and patience, not a goddamn exorcism! You have convinced yourself that they are bad children simply because they don't want to go to church? And just what kind of Christian does what you just did to them? Aren't you supposed to guide like Christ guided the lost? Where is the compassion? Anyone with God, truly in their hearts, would know this! Shame on you!"

Afterward, my Aunt Maria packed her things and left the house. My brothers and I did not see her again until quite some time had passed. We also did not step foot inside a church, nor did we become interested in anything having to do with religion for a long time. One could say that my aunt had left a lasting impression on us that none of us had a desire to relive.

CHAPTER 5

MEET THE BASTARDS

I was eleven years old the second time I went to El Salvador. I remember the second trip because it was so abrupt. One day, my brothers and I were being regular American kids, and then the next day, our father told us, "Pack your stuff. We're leaving for El Salvador in the morning. Don't pack any toys, just clothes. And if it can't fit in the luggage bag, then it's not going." My brothers and I had no choice but to process the announcement while we packed. Asking my father anything about the matter was out of the question as we knew that doing so would lead to us heading to El Salvador in pain.

Thinking back to my second experience in El Salvador, I can honestly say that I enjoyed it a lot better than my first trip. Albeit, we were there much longer than I had wished to stay, about a year. However, my family stayed in a sizeable house owned but not used by my uncle.

To my surprise, the house came with actual floors, functioning toilets, heating, air conditioning, and even a maid. What was even more exciting was that I got a room all to myself while my brothers had to share one. Obnoxiously, I made sure to rub that in their faces whenever I could. Another thing I enjoyed very much was that the maid had a daughter my age named Sofia. The two of us got along great from the moment we met.

Like the first time in El Salvador, I was once again helping my grandmother at her shop in the local market. Even though it had been six years since the last time I was there, not much had changed. The only real difference was that more shops had opened up, so the market seemed more populated than when I was there before.

Being eleven years old made my time at the shop harder since now all my grandmother saw was a bigger kid with more potential. She put me to work, unrooting and cleaning the various vegetables she sold at her shop. While the work was hard, at least harder than anything I had done back in the United States, I grew to enjoy it. Admittedly, I enjoyed it partly because I was getting paid that time around, and Sofia was there with me. Unfortunately for her, my grandmother did not pay her. Shockingly, Sofia did not mind it at all. At the time, I was her only friend, and she was my only friend. Spending the day together was enough for us.

One day, the market seemed more crowded and festive than it had ever been during the rest of my year there. Almost every shop was cooking some special dish or food item, and if the adults were not drinking, they were playing an instrument.

I would later find out that it happened to be El Salvador's Independence Day. Sofia could not be there with me because she had to help run her family's shop in another market. I remember the day being a "non-stop" sort of experience as there was no time for any breaks. It was washing, chopping, frying, and serving fried yuca, among other root vegetables. Afterward came the washing, squeezing, mixing, and serving of various fruit drinks. Finally, rolling up masa and cheese to make pupusas, a Salvadorian delicacy that my grandmother was famous for making. Lines of people gathered in front of her shop at just the smell of them cooking on the pan. Toward the end of the day, I felt like I had bathed in oil for hours on end.

I was finally relieved when some of my father's family showed up to help. They were also there to set up the fireworks station. My uncle was the wealthiest man in town, and so his fireworks station was the "go-to" place for fireworks on Independence Day.

Instead of taking advantage of the extended break I was on, I volunteered to help set up. Although I was familiar with what fireworks were, I had never been so close to them—especially the big ones. I remember lifting a giant firework that resembled a rocket up to my face so that I could closely inspect it. As I lowered it down to place it back into the box, that was when I saw them. The two "good-for-nothing bastards" ran off by my grandmother during my first visit to El Salvador.

"Poor boys, they were just looking for their father," I thought to myself at the time.

They were much older, but just like last time, they made their way over to my grandmother. Once they had gotten her attention, I instantly felt terrible for them. Judging by the look on my grandmother's face, they were in store for nothing good.

Suddenly, I heard a loud but familiar voice yell, "Hey Eden, get over here. Your uncle had a firework made just for you. Come see it!"

Filled with joy, I sprinted over to my father and hugged him once I reached him. "This one is going to explode big, and the colors will be pink and blue," he told me as he held me tight.

Once my father released me, I noticed that something had caught his attention behind me. Turning to look, I saw the two boys walking toward us.

"Go back to the shop, now." said my father sternly.

When I got there, I turned to look at my father and the two boys. Curious to know who exactly they were, I asked my grandmother. "Hey, Grandma, who are those two boys? Why are they talking with my father?"

Not pausing from slicing up the yuca, she said, "Those bastards are your brothers."

Upon hearing her response, I froze. All I could do was watch as my father and the two boys spoke. So many questions filled my head as I stood in silence.

"What are their names?" I asked my grandmother. At that moment, I knew that I had messed up.

She slammed down the knife and shouted, "Go ask your goddamn father!"

Startled by her response, I ran without hesitation toward my father. Arriving before him and the two boys, I asked, "Dad, are these boys my brothers?"

Upon hearing my question, my father burst out in laughter and replied, "No, no, I am their godfather. Who said I was their father?"

I told him that his mother had told me he was the boys' father, but he shrugged and said, "Your grandmother is old and crazy. Don't believe anything she tells you. Look, forget about that. The show is about to start."

As the fireworks went on, I could not help but become filled with joy. It had been a long time since I had seen my father happy and having fun.

Further, he was having fun with me. It was as if I had him all to myself. Conversely, I also could not dismiss the two boys who stood off toward the back and whose eyes did not watch the sky. Instead, their gazes stayed fixated on my father and me as we laughed, shouted, and danced the night away.

CHAPTER 6

ABOUT THAT BOY

Steven,

The first kid

Who was nice to me.

The first kid

Who did not judge me,

Based on my skin,

Or "poor" appearance.

He walked up to me

And said,

"Hello there, my name is

Steven,

Would you like to be friends?"

Steven,

The first kid

Who didn't repeat

The things his family

Said about people like me.

He walked up to me

And sat next to me in the schoolyard.

Sometimes we'd play,

Sometimes he'd let me read his comics,

And sometimes he'd even

Share his lunch with me.

Steven,

The first person my age,

To kiss me on the lips.

The first person

Whose kiss I welcomed

And enjoyed.

He walked up to me

And said,

"Hey, mi Hermosa,

Would you be my Valentine?"

Steven,

The first kid

I watched get beat up

By my brothers,

For liking me.

As they punched him

And kicked him,

He managed to get up

And run to his bike

And get away from them.

Steven,

The first person

To ever get hurt because of me.

Saying goodbye to him

Was the first time

I ever felt a stabbing pain in my heart.

And forgetting about him was nearly impossible.

But every once in a while,

I could not help but think

About that boy,

Steven.

CHAPTER 7

OUR LITTLE SECRET

"Just call me Adam," my uncle said to us as my brothers and I greeted him. He had just arrived from El Salvador and was going to live with my family until he became better situated.

Adam was not like any other of my father's brothers who had come up from El Salvador and lived with us. While they were all squares, Adam was full of laughter, rode a skateboard, blasted rock and roll music, and always found time to hang out with my brothers and me. My love for the Beatles stems from Adam, and even to this day, whenever I listen to a Beatles song, I cannot help but recall how he would turn up the volume and sing along with the music.

He was full of many fun stories from his youth. Unlike most of the grownups in my life at the time, Adam did not preach to me. He did not order my brothers and me around, nor did he lay his hands on us for "disciplinary" reasons.

Adam encouraged me to be different. "The world has too many boring people in it, Eden. Don't fall in line with boring; be different, be exciting."

One of the most memorable days we had with Adam was when we asked him to drive us around town. Junior had recently won a coupon book that could be used in stores and restaurants within the city to buy items at significantly discounted prices or get them for free. We must have driven around for hours, going from the comic book store to the toy store, then to Pizza Hut, 7-11, Shipley Do-Nuts, and many other places.

At one point, we were so full of all of the food we had eaten that we decided to stop at the park to sit and relax on the grass. However, we did not sit down for too long before we went to join a soccer game that was about to begin a few yards from us.

After the soccer game, we headed toward the car. Once inside, Adam turned to us and asked, "Have any of you ever driven before?"

Of course, my brothers and I thought he was kidding, but he was serious. Adam let Junior drive first and then Alex. I patiently waited my turn as they gently went around the parking lot, timid and scared.

Finally, I got behind the wheel. However, I would have to wait a little longer as Adam and my brothers adjusted the seat and strapped folded up magazines to the pedals to accommodate my short stature. Once I was sitting in front of the steering wheel, I knew that I wanted to outdo my brothers' boring driving.

"Okay, let me give you a quick—" Adam began to say before I rudely interrupted him by flooring the gas pedal without hesitation.

"Holy shit!" everyone in the car shouted as we sped down the straightest and longest strip of the parking lot.

Becoming excited, I began to do donuts with the car. Everyone just laughed and laughed. Suddenly, our laughter and excitement became terror as I lost control of the vehicle and crashed into a large plastic dumpster.

Having placed the car in park, Adam stepped out of the vehicle to observe the damage. Once he had walked a full circle around the car, he then headed toward me. Expecting to get smacked, I sat there and braced myself for impact. However, the hit never came.

"That was some crazy shit!" he shouted laughingly.

"You're not mad at me?" was all I could ask him.

"Mad at you for what? Oh, don't worry about the car. It's a piece of shit anyway. And none of you are hurt, right?" Adam calmly responded.

On the car ride back home, I could not help but think about what a gentle and fun person Adam was. I even vowed to be like him when I got older.

Arriving home, Adam parked the car, shut it off, and then turned to us and said, "Hey, me letting you guys drive the car today will be our little secret, okay?"

CHAPTER 8

WHO WE ARE

"Fuck the police coming straight from the underground...!" was all my father needed to hear to reach his boiling point. Although he very much enjoyed the song by the rap group NWA, it was eleven o'clock on a Sunday night and everyone in my house needed to wake up early the following day to either go to school or work. However, our next-door neighbors, a bunch of college students, did not seem to have a care in the world for who they were disturbing. They had been partying for the last two hours. During that time, they ignored the knocks of every neighbor who went to their door to complain.

"I'm going to go kick their fucking door down and smash that stereo system over their fucking heads!" shouted my father angrily as he walked out of the door and headed toward their house.

Curious to see what would happen, my family and I also made our way out to our front porch to watch. My father would not get the chance to enact his plan, however, as he veered his attention toward the sound of sirens and flashing red and blue lights coming his way. Realizing that it was the police, my father decided to wave them down.

Once they stopped and parked in front of the noisy neighbors' home, two police officers stepped out of the vehicle and walked toward the house.

"Hello, officers, I'm glad you guys are—" my father began to say before he was interrupted by one of the officers.

"We're not here to talk to you, so get the fuck out of the way before you get hurt," the officer sternly said to my father.

Confused by the police officer's demeanor toward him, my father just stood quiet.

"Ramirez, stay here and keep an eye on him," the officer told his partner as he walked up the front stairs of the neighbors' house.

While the rude police officer spoke with the noisy neighbors, my father thought it would be a good idea to talk with officer Ramirez.

"Hey, Ramirez, what's up with your partner? Why was he so rude? Hey, I'm not the bad guy here!" said my father.

Hearing my father speak to Officer Ramirez, the rude officer became perturbed and shouted, "Hey, Ramirez, tell that beaner to keep his fucking mouth shut, okay!"

"Yes, Sergeant O'Donnell," responded Officer Ramirez. "Look, be quiet until my sergeant is through with your neighbors. You're already off to a bad start, so listen to me if you don't want things to get worse."

Upon finishing his friendly conversation with the noisy neighbors, Sergeant O'Donnell then walked toward my father and Officer Ramirez.

"Okay, Pedro, they've turned down the music," said Sergeant O'Donnell to my father. "There's nothing to worry about anymore. They got a little carried away, but those are some good ol' American kids that live there, so leave them alone. Head back into your house and have a good night."

Confused but also clearly upset, my father could no longer hold in his anger. "First of all, my name is not Pedro, okay. And why the hell have you been such an asshole to me? I haven't done anything wrong!"

Unholstering his baton, Sergeant O'Donnell hastily walked toward my father, pointed his baton into his chest, and began to shout, "Being in my country is what you've done wrong, you filthy little wetback! You guys sneak into this country with your dirty-ass families and mooch off this country's wealth. All the while, forgetting your place here! You're scum, and the rest of those spics you got up there on your porch are also scum. It would benefit you a great deal never to forget that!"

I had hoped that my father would take his cue to turn around and come back into the house. Astonishingly, he did not. Puffing up his chest, he pressed on.

"Hey, you have no right to talk to me that way. I am an American. I did everything the right way so my family and I could be here! I also work hard, pay my taxes, and stay out of trouble. And with a name like O'Donnell, I'm pretty sure your ancestors came to this country just like I did. So, you come from immigrants as well!"

Upon hearing my father's message, Sergeant O'Donnell quickly grabbed his flashlight, turned it on, and pointed it at my father's face. Blinded by the bright beam of the flashlight, my father had no choice but to raise his hands to his eyes to shield them from the light.

Suddenly, Sergeant O'Donnell lunged at my father, whaling punches toward his head. As one connected, my father lost his balance and fell back onto the sidewalk. Everything happened so quickly; my mother, my brothers, my Uncle Adam, and I panicked and began to move toward my father to help him.

"Ramirez, keep them back! Point your fucking firearm at them; shoot them if you have to!" shouted Sergeant O'Donnell as he straddled my father and began to smash his face in with his fists.

A gun-toting Ramirez was all that stood between us and our father, between my mother and her husband, between Adam and his brother. No matter how much or how loudly we pleaded, our pleas fell on deaf ears. We had no choice but to stand there and watch as Sergeant O'Donnell attempted to make my father forever unrecognizable.

Out of breath from the barrage of punches he laid into my father's face, Sergeant O'Donnell finally stopped. "Ooh wee! This mother fucker looks like a fucked-up enchilada!" Sergeant O'Donnell shouted as he got up, turned around, and began walking toward the patrol car. "Come on, Ramirez, let's go get some tacos from Juanito's. I'm fucking starving!"

Once we saw Sergeant O'Donnell get into his vehicle, all of us sprinted toward our father as he lay on the sidewalk in a pool of blood. As the family sat there, Ramirez looked upon us with an expression as if to say "I'm sorry," but he could not say it.

Watching the patrol car drive off, we could not help but notice that our neighbors, from all directions, had witnessed the assault as well. However, like my family, they too had no choice but to stand by and let it happen.

As they began to head back into their homes, I looked to my mother and asked, "Why did they do this to Dad? They are the good guys, so why did they treat us this way?"

My mother could do nothing but cry as she held my dad in her arms.

"The ambulance is on their way," said Adam as he walked toward me with a blanket.

Wanting answers to my questions, I turned to Adam and asked him what I had asked my mother.

"Those two pieces of shit are not good guys, "Adam responded. "And that Sergeant O'Donnell asshole did what he did because of who we are."

"'*Who we are,*' what does that mean?" I thought to myself.

Some years would pass before I eventually learned what Adam had meant by "Who we are."

CHAPTER 9

GOODBYES & HELLOS

Goodbye, Dad,

I guess Mom grew tired

Of all the beatings.

She has decided to leave you

And take us with her.

Although I'll miss you,

I also don't want to keep

Seeing her with black eyes

Every time I kiss her.

I also don't want all

Of my earliest childhood memories

To be of you always

Yelling at and hitting Mom.

So, goodbye, Dad.

I love you.

Hello, Dad,

I'm so happy to see you.

I've missed you so much!

Even though Mom said

She'd had enough,

I guess she came to her senses.

She came to realize that on her own,

She can't provide

The shelter, food, and clothing

That my brothers

And I need.

I guess that night when

We all went to sleep hungry,

She saw that things

Were worse without you.

So now we're back!

Now that we're back,

Just promise me that

You'll treat her better

So we don't leave you again.

Goodbye, Dad,

I guess Mom grew tired

Of all the beatings

And of all the cheating.

She has decided

To leave you again.

And like last time,

She'll be taking us with her.

Although I'll miss you,

I also don't want to keep

Seeing her with black eyes

Every time I kiss her.

I also don't want all

Of my earliest childhood memories

To be of you always

Yelling at and hitting Mom

And my brothers.

I'm also getting pretty tired

Of always lying for you.

Even though you spoil me,

I don't want to have anything

To do with you

And your other women.

For once,

I'd like you to take me out

And for it to just be us

And not us and some other woman.

I don't know

If we'll ever get the chance,

But goodbye, Dad,

I love you.

Hello, Dad,

I'm so happy to see you.

I've missed you so much!

Even though Mom said

That she had enough,

I guess she came to her senses.

She came to realize that on her own,

She can't provide

The shelter, food, and clothing

That my brothers

And I need.

I guess that night when

We all went to sleep hungry,

She saw that things

Were worse without you.

I'm also sure that having

To hear shit from her older brothers

Instead of getting help from them

Became pretty tiring.

And Junior and Alex getting

Into constant trouble

Didn't help either.

She came to believe that

Those two needed fatherly guidance

To set them straight.

So now we're back!

Now that we're back,

Just promise me that

You'll treat her

And my brothers better

And that you won't make me

Lie for you anymore.

Please don't make me

Want to leave you as well.

Goodbye, Mom,

I guess you've grown tired

Of all the beatings

And of all the cheating.

So, you've decided

To leave Dad again.

However,

Unlike every other time before,

You won't be taking us with you.

So, I guess you've gotten

Quite tired of caring for us

All by yourself.

You must also need

Some time alone

To figure things out.

But don't worry, Mom,

I'm not mad at you one bit.

Go, do your thing

And don't worry about us.

I'll step up

And do things around the house.

And I'll make sure the boys

Stay out of trouble.

Don't you worry, Mom,

Things will be better

By the time you return.

I'll make sure of it.

Hello, Dad,

You're back from work early.

You're usually not back

Until late at night.

Well, I thought I'd cook us rice

Along with some chicken and peas.

Oh, God, Dad, you stink!

You've been drinking again,

Haven't you?

Well, the food should be... wait,

Dad,

What the hell are you doing?

Stop!

Get your hand out of my pants!

No! No! No!

Please, Dad, stop!

You're hurting me!

Why the fuck are you doing this?

I'm your daughter!

Please, stop, I'm begging you!

Why Dad?

Why?

Goodbye, Dad.

Even though I'm not there

To tell you in person,

I hope you know that we've left

You for good this time!

I hope you know that

No one will miss you, either.

As far as I'm concerned,

I wish you'd fucking die

And rot in hell

For what you did to me!

And to think that I was more concerned

With your wellbeing than mine!

That's why I didn't call the cops!

But now that I think about it,

I should have called them

So that they could've come

To beat the shit out of you

Like last time!

The only difference from the first time

Was that instead of screaming and crying,

Pleading with them not to kill you,

I would've laughed and cheered them on

The second time around!

I didn't call Mom, either,

Because she hadn't been

Gone long enough.

I didn't want to disturb her

As she tried to figure things out.

And I didn't tell my brothers

Because the thought

Of their ripped-up backs

Just wouldn't let me do it.

Do you see how,

Even after being a victim

Of your sick fuckery,

I still put my family first?

I was so full of love

For my family

And now I become sick

At the thought of being related to you!

God, I fucking hate you so much!

I hope that you know

That this isn't goodbye,

No, this is good riddance,

Mother fucker!

I hope that the next time

I see you

Is in a casket!

CHAPTER 10

THE BOSTON CELTICS

"Dammit, Brown, now's not the time to be fouling anyone!" shouted my Uncle Mike as he jumped out of his chair.

"Come on, bro, relax," responded Uncle Mike's best friend, Jorge. "Whether he fouls Tucker or not, the Celtics ain't pulling off a comeback in twenty seconds. Not with the Bulls leading by ten."

Sitting back down, it was clear that my uncle Mike had accepted the defeat. "Our boys just haven't been the same since Bird retired, man," he said as he changed the channel.

It was another night of us getting together to watch the Boston Celtics play on TV.

I loved those nights because they became filled with joyous shouting, good food, and overall togetherness. Although I had become accustomed to hearing shouting almost every night of my life, the kind that occurred on those nights was a lot different. Unless it was a member of the opposite team, no one in the house was being threatened with a beating, cursed at, or called derogatory names. Everyone in the house was having fun.

At the time, my brothers and I were in Boston, Massachusetts. We were living with my mother's brother, Mike. He had a lovely home and an even more delightful wife. My mother had been there since leaving my brothers and me with our father almost a year before.

On the road trip from Houston, Texas, to Boston, I honestly could not figure out if I would be happy to see my mother. After what had happened with my father, there were times that I became enraged at just the thought of my mother being elsewhere. There were even times when I blamed her for what had happened to me. I went as far as no longer writing to her, reading her letters, or talking to her on the phone. "What will I do or say to her?" I pondered. However, I soon found out as the truck pulled into the driveway and we saw our mother standing there waiting for us. My mother was in tears as soon as we got out of the truck, and so were we. We all became emotional and hugged each other so tightly.

"I've missed you guys so much," my mother said as she kissed each of us on the cheek.

Not knowing what to say, I let my brothers stay behind to talk to her as I helped Uncle Mike with our stuff.

Once everyone was in the house, Mike's wife Patricia greeted us with hot and fresh pupusas. As we sat and ate, we were in store for even more surprises. Family members I had never met before began pouring into the house. They greeted my brothers and me as if they had known us for years. Indeed, it was something to behold as my siblings and I had never received so many hugs, kisses, gifts, and money.

After all of the greetings, everyone headed to the dining room to enjoy even more of the delicious pupusas. As the afternoon turned into evening, the room became filled with stories and laughter. Although everyone had long finished eating, no one left the dining room as there was just too much fun going on. While everyone talked, I could not help but look around and appreciate what was happening around me. My entire family was genuinely happy. Becoming overwhelmed by it all, I began to cry. Not wanting to ruin the moment, I got up and sped off to the farthest bathroom.

However, I did not make it to the bathroom as my mother's voice stopped me.

"Hey, Eden, what's wrong?" she asked.

Frozen in my tracks like a deer in the headlights, I did not answer her. I turned around and faced her as she made her way toward me.

Once my mother reached me, she hugged me, looked at me, and began to say, "Listen, my baby girl. I know that you may be mad at me for leaving. And honestly, I don't blame you. I know things must have been rough for you and the boys without me there, but just know that leaving you guys was one of the hardest things I've ever done.

"There wasn't a day when I didn't think about you all. I missed you so much, and often, I would even think about going back. But I needed to leave. I needed to be as far away from your father as possible and with people who could help me. I came out here to start a new and better life for me, you, and the boys. For us!

"I don't know if you understand now, but I hope you can understand when you get older. It's all right. You can be mad at me, but I hope you can forgive me one day soon. I love you so much, Eden. I love you so much!"

Upon saying her piece, my mother hugged me and cried as I had never seen her cry before. Standing within my mother's loving embrace, I felt myself become weak. It was as if my legs had given out from under me. However, my mom was there. She felt me and began to hold me tighter.

"It's okay, baby. It's okay. I'm here," she said as I began to unleash a waterfall of tears onto her chest. A few minutes passed by before we released our embrace, looked at each other, and smiled. "Come on, let's go wash up," she said as she led me to the bathroom.

Once both of us no longer looked like we had been crying, we made our way back to the dining room. However, the dining room was not as packed as it was before I had left. It would not take long to find out where all of the men had gone. I heard a loud commotion coming from the living room. Before I headed over there, I turned to look at my mom sitting at the dining table talking with the other women. I waited until her eyes caught me, and then I smiled.

"What is going on in here?" I asked Uncle Mike as I entered the living room.

"Boston is about to play," he responded.

Confused by his response, I asked, "Boston, who?"

Astounded by what I had asked Mike, all the men turned their heads and shouted in unison, "The Boston Celtics!"

EPILOGUE

Do you know what it feels like

To be given

An unforgettable gift?

Do you know what it feels like

To play a game of

Hide & seek,

Only to have your life changed

Forever?

Do you know what it feels like

To scour every place you can think of

For as many coins as you can find

So you have enough money

To buy food

For you and your family?

Do you know what it feels like

To dress like a boy

So that you don't

Attract the attention

Of depraved men?

Do you know what it feels like

To watch someone

Possessed by the devil himself,

Try to snuff the life out of your brother?

Do you know what it feels like

To find out that you have brothers

In another land

That no one can seem

To give a shit about?

Do you know what it feels like

To have to say goodbye

To someone who cared about you

So dearly?

Do you know what it feels like

To have a cool uncle

Who never judges you

And who you build

A life-long bond with?

Do you know what it feels like

To watch the good guys

Beat up a family member

To within an inch of their life?

Do you know what it feels like

To wish, to hope,

And to pray so hard,

For something to be erased

From your fucking head?

Do you know what it feels like

To close your eyes,

Only to see someone

Grabbing your breasts,

Grabbing between your legs,

And ripping off your clothes,

To use every ounce of strength in your body,

To fight off someone

That is trying to rape you?

Do you know what it feels like

To have to live every day

Knowing that the person

Who tried to rape you

Is your own father,

To become sick to your stomach

Every day that you have

To live with the person

Who tried to rape you,

To have to try so hard

To never forget

To lock your bedroom door

Before going to sleep?

Do you know what it feels like

To not be able

To laugh or smile for months,

To become so angry

That you start blaming yourself

For something that was not your fault,

To want to set yourself on fire,

To want to jump off a bridge,

Or to want to swallow

An entire bottle of pills,

To hurt so bad

That you'd do anything

To make the pain stop?

Do you know what it feels like

To overcome pain and anger,

Only to replace it with hate,

To hate your father so much,

That you wish, you hope,

And you pray so hard

For something to happen to him

That would cause him great suffering?

Do you know what it feels like

To finally find happiness

After suffering through

What felt like an eternity

Of pain and sorrow?

Do you have any idea what it feels like?

To Be Continued

In...

PARADISE
THE DIARY OF EDEN FLORES PART II
BURNING

ACKNOWLEDGMENTS

First and foremost, I would like to thank you, Eden. Thank you for sharing your diary with me to explore the vital moments of your early life. It was indeed a pleasure to know that reading my first book encouraged you to share your story with someone. I will forever be blessed to have been the one with whom you chose to share a piece of your life.

To my Mom, Tia Loli, my brothers, Herbert Gonzalez and Gregory Brown, and my cousin, Delia, I love you all so dearly.

To my lovely wife, Arjelle Lawrence, thank you for loving me and being my rock.

To those of you who have chosen to read this book, thank you!

ABOUT THE AUTHOR

Omar Gonzalez is a former member of the US Armed Forces and is currently a Doctor of Physical Therapy. More notably, Omar is also an award-nominated author, having released his first book, *The Phantom Struggle: Memoirs of a Life Once Struggling*, in the late summer of 2020.

The product of a turbulent, alcohol-ridden, and low-income home, he has been homeless and was not afforded the opportunity of having an all-around safe and fun childhood. However, when speaking to him directly, he would never disclose such information. Instead, Omar would like for people to read about his various experiences in life. Whether it is encountering abuse, love, heartache, religion, or self-discovery, he has a poem or story for such an experience.

When he is not busy with professional endeavors, Omar spends his time thinking of ways to write about his life or others' lives and does not shy away from using fantastic elements to convey his message. Omar yearns to write emotion-driven stories that captivate the readers' spectrum of emotions and imagination so that they feel and see the story unfold before them.

WHAT DID YOU THINK?

First of all, thank you for purchasing *Paradise Taken*. I know you could have picked any number of books to read, but you chose this book, and for that, I am incredibly grateful. I hope it added some value and quality to your everyday life. If so, it would be nice if you could share this book with your friends and family by posting about it on any social media platforms you may use.

If you enjoyed this book and found some benefit in reading it, I would like to hear from you and hope that you could take some time to post a review on Amazon, Barnes & Noble, or wherever you may have purchased the book. I want you to know that your review is critical. Your feedback and support will significantly improve my writing craft for future projects and make this book even better. I wish you all the best in your life, and once again, thank you!

PLEASE REACH OUT TO ME ON SOCIAL MEDIA!

 josue.omar.g@gmail.com

 @doc_omar_g

 @Omar.G.2020

 @Doc_OmarG

www.ingramcontent.com/pod-product-compliance
Lightning Source LLC
Chambersburg PA
CBHW070106070426
42448CB00038B/1831